How to Write a Screenplay That Doesn't Suck (and Will Actually Sell)

Vol.1 of the ScriptBully Screenwriting Collection

by Michael Rogan
Editor, ScriptBully Magazine

Published in USA by: ScriptBully Magazine

Michael Rogan

© Copyright 2016

ISBN-13: 978-1-970119-00-8

Table of Contents

About the Author

Michael Rogan is a former Hollywood screenplay reader, optioned screenwriter and editor of ScriptBully magazine - an inbox periodical devoted to helping screenwriters write well...and get paid.

He is also the owner of the world's most neurotic Jack Russell Terrier.

And has made it his mission in life to rid the world of movies about trucks that turn into robots.

A Special FREE Gift for You!

If you'd like FREE instant access to my seminar "7 Secrets to a Kick-Ass and Marketable Screenplay" then head over to ScriptBully.com/Free. (What else you gonna do? Watch another "Twilight" movie?!)

Prologue: "Got a Feeling We're Not in Kansas Anymore"

There's a nasty secret about the film business nobody wants you to know.

And that is....

There's nobody stopping you. Read that again.

There's NOBODY stopping you.

Newbie screenwriters think industry insiders spend countless hours coming up with diabolical ways to keep them out.

"We'll make them send query letters on embossed letterhead we never read."

"We'll make them buy hundred-dollar memberships to industry-endorsed networks we never visit."

"We'll make them enter contests nobody on earth actually pays attention to...Wha-Ha-ha!"

Are you kidding? They want you.

Like a Kardashian sister in search of the paparazzi, the film biz desperately wants to "discover" your awesome, amazing script and help you cultivate your talent into an unstoppable force of story awesomeness.

And it's got nothing to do with being generous or supportive or artistic.

It's because they get credit for DISCOVERING you.

They don't get bonus points for hiring Steve Zallian or Eric Roth.

They don't get a corner office for buying another Christopher Nolan "vehicle."

They don't get a better table at The Ivy because they signed on for "Fast and Furious Part 10: More

Furiousness."

"I Coulda Been a Contender"

Studio executives and agents and producers ASCEND the Hollywood hierarchy ladder if they discover the next Diablo Cody. The next Alexander Payne.

The next...you!

When they do that, they get a promotion. And believe me, there's nothing these assholes like more than a promotion.

But to get discovered...

To sell your screenplay for close to $500,000 and have insanely expensive lunches in Century City and buy overpriced Italian sports cars that get four miles to the gallon and date leggy super models named Ivanka....

You have to "act" like a professional.

You have to "talk" like a professional.

You have to "write" like a professional.

And the only way to do that is to take the craft, and the business, of screenwriting seriously.

That's what this book is all about.

"You're Gonna Need a Bigger Boat"

Now...you could go to *film school* and spend *$125,000 on a film degree* that teaches you how to write unsellable films about Depression-era potato farmers.

Or you could *stalk Judd Apatow at the Santa Monica Whole Foods* until he reads your 150-page script about college students on a road trip to Wichita.

Or you could enter every screenwriting contest on the face of the Earth, hoping the *Tucson High-Desert Ladies Auxiliary Screenplay Hootenanny* helps you get an agent.

Or...you could follow the 10 tricks in this book to help you BOOST your screenwriting know-how, WRITE a kick-ass screenplay and then put yourself in a great position to actually...you know...make a frickin' living off your words.

I can't promise you'll sell a script by following these 10 steps. (Not only would it be unethical, but I'm sure the FCC would throw me in self-published prison.)

But I can promise if you commit to the steps I've outlined, you will:

- *Know more about screenplay structure than 99 percent of the screenwriters out there. (And that includes the ones who get paid.)*

- *Accelerate your knowledge of the film business from naive wannabe to seasoned film industry veteran, virtually overnight.*

- *Learn an email query template for approaching managers and agents in a professional way that works. (And by works, I mean it gets your frickin' script read!)*

- *Discover ninja secrets to being perceived as a*

professional, and not some noob working at Home Depot.

- *Be THAT much closer to converting your talent into an insanely marketable asset that lets you quit your job, sneer at your enemies and...rule the world!*

As Yogi Berra said, "You can observe a lot just by watchin'." And what better to watch than the movies?

So...let's get started. Shall we?

Chapter 1:
Embracing Your Inner S-O-B

"Most of the shadows of this life are caused by our standing in our own sunshine."

-Ralph Waldo Emerson

I know what the screenwriting books say. That you need a main character for your story that's likable. Relatable. Empathetic.

Sorry. But that's to-tal horse shit!

Rooster Cogburn (John Wayne) in "True Grit" is a bitter, obese sociopath. Popeye Doyle (Gene Hackman) in "The French Connection" is a corrupt, maniacal police officer willing to do ANYTHING to catch his target. Michael Coreleone (good, old Al Pacino) in "The Godfather" — is the MOST evil person in a story filled with folks who decapitate horses and send dead fish parcels.

You do NOT have to center your stories around relatable characters who are kind to puppies, test well with focus groups and would pass a Government-mandated background check.

In fact — in these morally murky and economically uncertain times — I believe the less conventional and empathetic your main character, the better.

But...your hero MUST have one thing: Drive.

And frickin' LOTS of it.

Your hero must be driven — whether by greed, jealousy, revenge, an obsession with Chinatown or a belief that "men and women can't be friends" — to sacrifice MORE and compromise LESS than anybody else in your story. (And that includes your villain.)

Because the only way your hero will scratch the surface of their potential as a compelling story character — and overcome all the crazy, insane obstacles you will put in their way — is to be mad. Obsessed. Uncompromising. Driven.

This doesn't mean your hero needs to be a raving lunatic or get into a shouting match in every scene. (We aren't writing a community college one-act play.)

But it means they NEED to have an obsessive drive to gain something tangible, and be prepared to let nothing — even themselves — stand in their way.

"I'm Gonna Make Him an Offer He Can't Refuse"

The trouble us writers have in creating driven, obsessed characters is…well…we're writers.

We like to stay in the shadows. Peek behind the curtain. Hide behind our Dell laptop and triple-shot lattes.

We aren't (usually) type-A folks — unless our name is Joe Esterzhas — and we often see life in shades of nuance and ambiguity.

Which is great: This sensitivity to the nuance and ambiguity of life makes us the perfect vehicle for great stories. (And why professional athletes and talk-show hosts make such shitty writers.)

But save the nuance and the ambiguity for your third act. Or your 14th rewrite.

When you're in the trenches of early story development, it's best to make bold creative choices. And the best way I know how to do this is to find that inner SOB inside you that's just dying to get out. (Don't worry, there'll be plenty of people to tame your inner hell-beast later.)

So, here are FOUR tips to help you find passionate, uncompromising characters that'll make perfect vehicles for your story:

Inner SOB Tip No.1: What's YOUR Chinatown?

Most (good) stories start from some kind of obsession or strong belief the writer has. So start off by asking yourself:

- What the hell makes me driven?

- What would I be willing to give up everything for?

- What do I THINK is worth stepping on toes, ruffling feathers and kicking serious ass to accomplish?

And, please, try to make it specific. I know you're passionate about FREEDOM and JUSTICE. And, though commendable, those are vague and un-filmable concepts.

Go deeper, get emotional. Maybe it's "putting serial rapists behind bars," or "spying on the neighbors because you're convinced they're Communists" or "ridding the world of any movies based on a Milton Bradley board game."

Action Step: Come up with a list of at least THREE topics you feel STRONG about and would force you to step way outside your comfort zone to achieve.

Inner SOB Tip No.2: Turn the Volume Knob Up to 11

Now it's time to go to light speed. For each of your three topics, take those topics to their most logical — and illogical — extreme.

- What would a character passionate about this topic, and with absolutely no compromise in their DNA, do?

- How would they talk?

- What do they obsess about?

- What's their apartment look like?

- How are their personal and professional relationships?

- What do they feel is the ONLY,

reasonable thing for them to do?

Does your main character hunt paroled rapists on the street vigilante-style with a crossbow? Or does your main character convert their studio apartment into an ad hoc surveillance center?

Action Step: Try to come up with two or three different character variations — and what they feel they HAVE to accomplish. The more obsessed and extreme you go with these characters, the better. Your story (and your pocketbook) will thank you.

Inner SOB Tip No.3: Give 'Em a Crazy, Hectic Job

This one may seem unimportant, but it shocks me how many newbie screenwriters will give their main character — you know, the person they hang all 97 pages of their story on — some boring, and visually uninteresting, occupation.

Like professor. Or actor.

Or writer.

Trust me: NOBODY cares about writers. (In fact, most people resent how much "free time" they think we have.)

And unless that professor, actor or writer also is obsessed with nuclear launch codes or the whereabouts of the kidnapped president or the unjust murder of their roommate...

Then leave the "desk job" until AFTER you get your three-picture deal at Universal. Instead, pick an occupation — or story world — that promises:

- Visual Conflict

- Constant Tension

- Numerous Obstacles

- Bureaucracies (Of any kind)

- Lots and Lots of Problems

And when I say "job," I don't mean this literally. Being a housewife is a job. Running the church bake sale is a job. Caring after your disabled parent is a job.

Just make sure you choose something fraught with conflict and tension. (And bonus points if it's a "job" world that you know something about.)

Action Step: Come up with 2-3 occupations for your main character that promises (visual) conflict.

Inner SOB Tip No.4: Put a Fork in the Road

Now you've got a passionate, obsessed character — with a hard-core, visually interesting work or home environment...

It's now time to put someone — or something — in their way. Namely your villain, your baddie, your antagonist.

Your main opposition to the main character.

Now this character doesn't have to be evil or maniacal...or even human. They need to STAND directly in the way of what your opponent wants. Either by a) wanting to acquire the SAME THING your main character wants or b) wanting to derail your main character at every turn.

Either way, crafting a good opponent is the GLUE of your story. It's also the most fun you'll have as a screenwriter. (And lets you plumb your Freudian sadistic tendencies.)

Because THIS opponent is your main character's worst nightmare. And like every nightmare they come from somewhere deep in the consciousness of the person dreaming.

But the opponent has to CRAFTED to hit your main character where it hurts. Darth Vader is an awesome villain for Luke Skywalker. (Half-robot dictator vs. Rural farm boy) But notice how different that battle would be if it was Darth Vader squaring off against Han Solo? Or Michael Coreleone? Or Dirty Harry? (Not so bueno.)

So, come up with two or three obsessed, uncompromising opponents who will bring out the best — and worst — in your main characters. Doing this will make things like screenplay structure and act breaks and story construction a hell of a lot easier.

(Which is what we'll cover in the next chapter.)

Action Step: Come up a kick-ass opponent that stands directly in the way of what your character wants.

Chapter 1 Key Takeaways:

- Brainstorm three topics, or issues, you have little compromise over. Express it as something you feel SHOULD be done. Be specific.

- Create two or three characters based on hyper exaggerated versions of these issues. Go as far as you can with it.

- Come up with visually interesting occupations for each of these character variations. Avoid writers at your creative peril.

- For each character, construct an equally obsessed opponent who can stand in their way at every turn. Be sure the opponent only WINS if your hero loses.

Chapter 2:
Stop Waiting for Perfect

"Perfection is the enemy of excellence."

-Voltaire

I'm reminded of something Susannah Grant, world-class screenwriter of "Erin Brockovich" — and "In Her Shoes," told me at a conference a few years back. I asked her what her approach to screenwriting structure was:

"Have something big happen every 10 pages."

That was it.

No Act-II Midpoint. No detailed character studies. No 57-step outline with graphs and pie charts and index cards laid out on a cork board from

Staples.

Now Ms. Grant has a ton of box office hits and acres of New Mexico property to back this up.

But many professional screenwriters don't wait until they have every nuance and bit of story structure worked out before they WRITE.

They get just enough to start and then they get rolling.

And they don't stop until they have a first draft.

"No Wire Hangers!"

Shane Black, writer of "Lethal Weapon," thinks waiting to write until you have a Syd-Field type framework is "lame and unproductive."

"It's all set-ups, payoffs and reversals," believes Black. "The rest is bullshit."

But what about your *outline?*

Your *12-page beat sheet?*
That *256-page color-coded treatment* you've spent

nineteen months on?

Those are fine. Like Dumbo and his feather, whatever helps you get started is cool.

Just as long as you get started.

But if you spend most of your time preparing to write and not enough time actually writing - and you know who you are - below is all the structure you really need.

And you don't have to take a $350 Lew Hunter learning annex class to learn it. (I know, because I did. And it was awful.)

Structure Tip No.1: Have a MAJOR Reversal or Turning Point Every 10 Pages

Example: Obi-Wan is killed. Harry and Sally sleep together. Vampires play baseball.

By building these turning points into your scripts - and making sure each of those 10 pages is building toward that reversal - you'll have just enough "spine" or "structure" in your script to get written. (But not too much structure you'll lose interest in your script.)

And forget all that three-act bull crap.

Viewers don't experience movies thinking, "Oh, I love the way they're resolving this Act-II dilemma."

They experience events like a roller coaster.

Up-up-up-up...then downnn! Then up again. Then down again.

Then they get off the ride, go home and complain about the price of the popcorn.

You will naturally, in the course of writing, gravitate towards a "structure" that fits your story.

But if you insist on making your story fit into some rigid control-freak box, your reader will see it coming.

And they'll never get to that awesome Act-II midpoint you've spent years working on.

Structure Tip No.2: Give Every Scene a Minor Reversal

Meaning: if the scene starts happy, *end sad*. If it starts sad, have it *end upbeat*.

Make the scene DO something, GO somewhere.

I know a successful screenwriter who makes sure the end of every scene he writes warrants that grave-sounding "Duh-Duh-Duh" musical stinger that old radio soap operas used to have.

"Downton Abbey" does this well. So does every episode of "Law and Order." (The original series, not the crappy SVU spin-offs.)

It's just a modern version of the old Saturday morning serial cliffhanger.

And it's just good storytelling: Leave the viewer wanting/dying to know what happens next.

As a script reader, I'm emotionally involved in a script if I NEED to know what happens next.

And scripts that do this consistently will make

you *wealthier than you can imagine.*

Clue: The way to achieve this is often by writing less, not more. (But we'll get to that later.)

Meaning: if the scene starts happy, *end sad.* If it starts sad, have it *end upbeat.*

Make the scene DO something, GO somewhere.

I know a successful screenwriter who makes sure the end of every scene he writes warrants that grave-sounding "Duh-Duh-Duh" musical stinger that old radio soap operas used to have.

"Downton Abbey" does this well. So does every episode of "Law and Order." (The original series, not the crappy SVU spin-offs.)

It's just a modern version of the old Saturday morning serial cliffhanger.

And it's just good storytelling: Leave the viewer wanting/dying to know what happens next.

As a script reader, I'm emotionally involved in a script if I NEED to know what happens next.

And scripts that do this consistently will make you *wealthier than you can imagine.*

Clue: The way to achieve this is often by writing less, not more. (But we'll get to that later.)

Structure Tip No.3: Pick a Main Character Who Has a Mortal Fear

We touched on this in the last chapter. But it's important your main character not just have a STRONG BELIEF about something such as:

- *Men and women can't be friends ("When Harry Met Sally")*

- *It's better to look out for yourself and stay neutral in war time ("Casablanca")*

- *Money can buy love ("Citizen Kane")*

But they need to have a MORTAL FEAR. Usually, but not always, related to them NOT getting their belief satisfied.

And it can be anything they're afraid of:

- *Snakes*
- *Commitment*
- *Chinatown*
- *Prison*
- *Loneliness*
- *Sex*
- *Germs*
- *The Government*
- *Being Ordinary*

It's your job to do everything you can to force them to face that fear. Literally.

If they're afraid of germs, *trap them in an elevator with a Boy Scout troop.* If they're afraid of commitment, *force them to get married in 30 days,* or they will lose their inheritance. If they're afraid of living without money, make them *lose everything and have them go live in a hippie commune in Vermont.* (Can't you just see Tim Allen in the lead?)

By doing this, and seeing how your character reacts, your script will display all those buzzwords that development executives love: growth, change, depth, and relate-ability. And you won't have to put in some crappy scene where your main character saves a puppy from a burning building.

The MORE you can link up the erroneous belief and the mortal fear, the more character gold you'll have in your script.

Structure Tip No.4: Put 10 "Open Loops" Into Your Script (and Make Them Pay Off)

The human brain is funny. It loves questions and puzzles and riddles. (Overpriced therapists call these *open loops.*)

But if you don't close open loops, people get really frustrated.

This is why any self-help guru will tell you asking yourself questions that have specific, clear answers are healthier than asking yourself open-ended questions that don't have a clear response.

Example: "Why can't I write anything good?" has a much different impact on your psyche than asking "How can I get better at writing today?"

And when people are watching your movie or reading your script they are constantly asking questions:

- *Why is that guy wearing a black hat?*

- *Does she know that man in the restaurant?*

- *Will that gun show up later?*

- *She gave him a look. Will that be important later?*

- *Will the girl and the piano player end up together?*

Most people ask these questions to themselves. People like my wife will wonder what the hell is going on every minute of a movie.

Point is: When you pay these off over the course of your story, magic happens.

Because...it REWARDS the viewer for paying attention. Open loops can include:

Repeated Dialogue:

- *"I made him an offer he couldn't refuse."*
- *"You complete me."*
- *"Go ahead, make my day."*

Same Location, Different Result:

- *Julia Roberts in "Pretty Woman" returning to the Rodeo Drive store that turned her down.*
- *Michael Corleone being embraced as the new Godfather, in the same office his Dad resided over.*
- *Tom Hanks returning to the fortune-teller booth in "Big."*

Physical Objects:

- *The spinning top in "Inception."*
- *The cattle gun in "No Country for Old Men."*
- *The bat signal in "Batman."*

Symbols:

- *Butterflies in "Silence of the Lambs."*
- *Food in "The Help."*
- *The color red in "Carrie."*

Don't over-think this. You're not writing "My Dinner With Andre." You're just giving your reader/viewer some mental popcorn. Believe me, they'll love you for it.

Yes, there's a lot more to screenplays than that. Yes, you COULD spend months, if not years, working on your treatment. Yes, there's so much more to writing like a pro.

But I firmly believe screenwriting is like driving. It's hard to learn how to parallel park from an owner's manual. (And nearly impossible if you never start the car.)

Chapter 2 Key Takeaways:

- Have a MAJOR turning point in your story every 10 pages. Don't obsess about act breaks; just concentrate on building toward your turning points.

- Try to have each scene end on a reversal (of some kind.) If the scene starts happy, end sad…and vice versa.

- Pick ACTIVE main characters who have terrifying fears. Bonus points if it's something you're afraid of.

- Add at least 10 open loops to your story. Whether that be lines of dialogue, symbols, objects, places…or whatever.

Chapter 3:
Reading, Writing and (Movie) Arithmetic

"I like to work half a day. I don't care if it's the first twelve hours or the second twelve hours."

-Kemmons Wilson

I know. Reading scripts.

Sounds about as much fun as watching "High School Musical."

Again.

But it's only by reading countless scripts, both good ones and bad ones, that you learn the rhythm of a screenplay.

This is especially true within a genre you hope to work in.

If you write horror, you have to know how horror scenes read.

THWACK! and SLICE! and ZWOOM! intermeshed in the description is perfectly acceptable for a spec about zombies. Not so much for a gritty espionage drama.

If you're writing a romantic comedy, you have to know the ancient rule of "write only what you see" is total bullshit.

Description like the following may not be poetry, but it's kosher within the rom-com genre:

INT. QUIRKY APARTMENT - DAY.

JAMIE, 22, vacuums her apartment. She's pretty, smart, driven. The kind of girl who's kept a wedding scrapbook since the womb.

Besides, if you read enough bad scripts (like I have), you'll appreciate when a writer knows what the hell they're doing. (So will agents and production company readers.)

And between 90-105 pages, you can easily dust off a script a week by reading 15-20 pages a day. (What the hell else are you going to do in the bathroom at work?)

Where the Wild Things Are

A good place to find free scripts — although this can change due to copyright issues - is SimplyScripts.com.

I like to print them out. (I hate reading stuff on a screen.) But that's just me.

Whatever you do, don't print them out at Kinko's. They're the Mafia of the printing industry and will extort you in service charges.

What I do is reach out to local printers to see if they'll make me a deal. (i.e., if you send them a 120-page script a week to print, what will they charge you?)

Usually you can get a 120-page script for $6. (Dirt-cheap, and well worth the investment in your filmic knowledge.)

Other screenwriters won't don't do this. It's too much work. It costs too much money. They don't want to drive to the store.

And yet doing this will make you a MUCH better writer. Fast.

For those Uber-lazy types, you can head over to Amazon and get a used copy of a screenplay for just a couple bucks.

Here are three scripts every self-respecting screenwriter should have in their library:

"Moonstruck"
John Patrick Shanley

Great, believable dialogue. Interesting, complex characters. And some of the best handling of multiple sub-plots you'll ever see.

Amazon link:

http://scriptbully.com/moonstruck

"Shawshank Redemption"

Frank Darabont

Yes, Shawshank is one of the best American films of the last 50 years. But it's also some of the most subtle voice-over writing ever done. Worth picking up a copy to see how Frank Darabont handles this.

Amazon link:
Http://scriptbully.com/shawshank

"Raising Arizona"

Joel and Ethan Coen

Probably my favorite Coen film of all time; this quirky offbeat comedy does a great job of setting up the entire premise of the film. In three pages. Amazing.

Amazon link:
Http://scriptbully.com/arizona

And something magical happens when you read scripts on a regular basis. The visual, film-y type style of screenwriting seeps into your writing. (Almost without trying.)

You can't read this bit from Saving Private Ryan and not have it HELP make you a better writer.

```
EXT. OMAHA BEACH - NORMANY -
DAWN

    Huge fifteen-inch guns.

SWARM OF LANDING CRAFT

    Heads directly into a
nightmare. MASSIVE EXPLOSIONS from
German artillery shells and mined
obstacles tear apart the beach.

    Boys. Most are eighteen or
nineteen years old. Tough. Well-
trained. Trying to block out the
surrounding fury.
```

Damn. That's good. (And doable, if you continue to read them scripts.)

"I'll Have What She's Having"

Okay, let's talk writing. Namely doing it…every day.

This is non-negotiable. Sorry. To be a professional writer, you must write every day. (And yes, that means Saturdays and Sundays.)

Notice I didn't say how much.

Some writers, like Oscar-winning screenwriter Paul Haggis, have a daily goal of five pages a day.

When he reaches that goal, he's done for the day and can go spend his millions of dollars taking down the Church of Scientology.

Other writers, like Stephen King, block their time in hourly chunks.

When Mr. King hits 2:30 p.m. — no matter how much he's written — he knows it's time to turn off the computer and see how badly his Red Sox are playing.

You could do five pages, two hours, 45 minutes,

a scene, 250 words. Whatever.

The key is to do it *every day*. To make it routine. A ritual.

"Say 'Hello' to my Little Friend"

Ideally, I would start with a page a day and work up from there. Anybody can do a page. Even the laziest, procrastination-infected layabout can muster a page.

Best of all, at a page a day you'll have three-and-a-half scripts done in a year. (See if your slacker film-nerd friends can say the same.)

And a page a day is just to START.

You might get cookin' and keep rolling through to three pages. But whatever your amount, make sure you meet the minimum. (Or I'll come find you and make you watch the extended edition of "Gigli.")

Just don't make it a superhuman goal only Shakespeare or Aaron Sorkin could reach. Yes, 10 pages a day would be nice, but there's no way you'll be able to keep it up over the long haul.

And you'll just end up getting frustrated and hating yourself. (Don't worry, there's plenty more opportunities for self-hatred as a writer.) This just doesn't have to be one.

"We'll Always Have Paris"

And if you absolutely can't think of what to write, then just write about NOT being able to write.

Trust me, after a while your sub-conscious mind will get SO bored it'll want to write just to shut you up.

If I can't think of anything, I'll just write something like this:

```
INT. CAFE - DAY.

Michael Rogan, 48, famous
screenwriter and the object of
women's affection around the
world, sits at the desk of his
evil lair/writer's office.
```

MICHAEL
But what if everything I do is
shit? What if I did my best work
ten years ago?

LINSDAY LOHAN
(O.S.)
I don't let it stop me.

And if you still can't get yourself motivated to write every day - even with Lindsay Lohan as your muse - then just steal a page from that famed productivity expert, Jerry Seinfeld.

Yeah, that *Jerry Seinfeld.*

The world-class comedian had a system, when he was first starting out in stand-up, for making himself write jokes every day.

He put up a board on his wall that had a square for each day. And if he wrote a certain amount of jokes that day, then he got to put an 'x' through that day's square.

Funny thing happened.

His motivation for writing jokes wasn't tied to

fame or career or world domination. It was about not breaking that chain of 'x's.

You could do a whole lot worse than creating your own chain of screenwriting x's.

Chapter 3 Key Takeaways:

- Try your best to READ a screenplay each week. Grab a copy from Simply Scripts or from Amazon and read 10-15 pages a day. (Preferably scripts in your chosen genre...and written in the last 10 years.)

- Decide on a realistic daily page or writing time quota. And STICK TO IT! At a page a day, you could have a rough draft of your script in three months.

Chapter 4:
What Stale Popcorn Can Teach You About Writing

"Don't be satisfied with stories. Unfold your own myth."

-Rumi

I know. You're busy. You've got *things to do.*

And the going to the movies is SO expensive. And the parking horrendous. And the popcorn overpriced.

And where the hell did these stupid kids come from?

And on and on...

Thing is: It's hard to be captivated by a movie while you're eating dinner and checking your cell phone and updating your Facebook status…

…and listening to your neighbors fight over the bong….

It's like a professional violin player saying: "Do I need to go to the symphony when I've got the CD at home?"

Sometimes you just gotta be there.

Besides you're not just going for the movie. You're going for *market research.*

- You're going to see what the trailers are like. Are they selling the story or the stars? Hint: Stars aren't as prominent in marketing as they used to be.

- You're going to see what the posters in the lobby say. How is tone conveyed in the poster? Is the "spine" of the story clear or is it more abstract? Hint: It depends on genre.

- You're going to see who the target audience of a poster or trailer is. There was a time when films tried to appeal to everyone. NO LONGER. With "The Hangover" and "Sex and the City," studios recognized that people go see movies with their friends, and oftentimes leave their spouses at home.

- You're going to see, in real-time, how people are reacting to these promotional items. Does Eddie Murphy surrounded by Ritalin-fueled four-year-olds make YOU want to see that film? How 'bout that family of four sitting next to you?

- You're going to see, in real-time, who actually GOES to movies. Look around the lobby of a movie theater. Do you think your script about a depressed writer and his quirky, but troubled ex-girlfriend will interest these moviegoers? Or do you think a movie about a computer hacker who must break into the Pentagon and steal a hard drive or the Russian Mafia will kill his girlfriend, might be a bit more interesting to that family of five.

- You'll find out WHO studios are making movies with and the genres of those movies. You'll learn Columbia Pictures, for stupefying reasons, continues to work with Adam Sandler and his production company Happy Gilmore. They may not be the best studio to approach about your Edwardian period drama.

- And…you'll learn what you shouldn't spend months working on. Many screenwriters think it's great that a similar idea is getting made, rather than realizing they've been beaten to the screenwriting punch.

And if you're feeling particularily, super-ninja then you could even talk to actual human beings, your fellow movie-goers. And you could ask them things like:

- Why did they choose the movie they chose?
- What trailers are THEY excited about?
- What's the most important element they look for in the movies they chose? (If they say "who's in it," pin them down. What is it about the stars they like?)

You could even pitch them your story idea if you're feeling especially brave. (I know, perish the thought.)

But movie studios spend millions of dollars each year on focus group research that isn't 10% as effective as this. (And all it will cost you is a $7 matinee ticket and a box of Milk Duds.)

And before you tell me you're writing a non-commercial, indie film that doesn't stoop to such pedantic levels as trying to reach the masses…save it!

Good movie marketing isn't about writing some shitty script that looks a hell of a lot like a Michael Bay trilogy.

It's about respecting your audience. Realizing people are busy, and they have a hell of a lot of other things to do. And if you start to think like a studio marketing department, you'll realize that making extreme story choices isn't cheesy or commercial or selling out.

It's good business. (And contrary to what your film studies professor wants you to believe, this is definitely a business.)

So…ask yourself?

What would my script's poster be?

If I couldn't get Steve Carell or Scarlet Johansson to star in my movie (and if you can, then why the hell are you doing reading this?) how would a trailer get people to see my film?

What would I need to express in terms of title, tone, image and headline to make people fight their distrust of new things and go see that movie?

Then go write that film.

Chapter 4 Key Takeaways:

- Commit to seeing a movie in the theater three or four times a month. Become a student of movie marketing. (And buttered popcorn.)

- Pay attention to everything. The trailers, the lobby posters, the cardboard cutouts, the actual paying audience that shows up.

- Imagine what the poster of your movie would look like. What about your story could grab total strangers to pay money for your story?

Chapter 5:
The Ultimate $9.99 Film School

"The length of a film should be directly related to the endurance of the human bladder."

-Alfred Hitchcock

This might be the most important tip in this entire book.

I guarantee if you add this to your weekly routine, you will know more about film structure than 99 percent of the other schmucks who send scripts in to be considered.

And that's because it takes time.

And nobody likes to do anything that takes time. Ever. (Too many stupid iPhone games to play.)

But consciously watching a movie, with a screenplay in your hands, is one of the most effective ways to LEARN the craft of screenwriting.

Here's how it works:

Each week, choose a film that's out on DVD or saved to your DVR. (Preferably something in your genre and produced in the last 10 years.)

Print out a screenplay of that film. (Check out SimplyScripts.com or just do a Google search of the film title and the word "PDF.")

Watch the film side-by-side with the script, breaking down the script scene-by-scene, making notes of what's working and what's not.

Here's what to look for:

- Did the director "remove" pieces of the script from the final version? If so, why? Hint: Cutting stuff makes things better.

- Notice how setting and location are often used as a force of antagonism and not just a "place" to put the camera. Whether it's the desert in "Lawrence of Arabia" or the seedy underbelly of the city in

"Seven," the setting should provide challenges and conflicts for your main character at every level.

- Look for how the writer deals with exposition: Is it in a boring, straightforward manner, or used as a weapon by one character against another? (Woody Allen is the king of expositional warfare, especially in "Annie Hall" and "Husbands and Wives.")

- Determine how the script description conveys emotional information actors can use. Description isn't about where to put the camera, it's about helping people "see" what you "see." (And that includes actors and directors.)

- Assess which scenes you like. Watch them again to see why. Usually there's a feeling of equally matched "opponents" squaring off. (Or it's got Natalie Portman in it. Either one.)

- Evaluate which scenes you don't like. Watch these again to see where the script falls flat. Usually it's because they're over-written with nothing clear at stake. (Or they've got Kirsten Dunst in them. Either one.)

- Most importantly: Notice where a scene changes; where it shifts direction, how characters go in thinking one way, then have to keep re-adjusting to what happens in the scene to get what they want.

- Make note of what page number BIG events, such as act breaks, mid-points and climaxes, happen. I know what the Syd Field books say — that Act I should happen about page 30 — but attention spans have undergone a strict diet since then. And chances are, you'll need to get to the good stuff much quicker than a previous generation.

It should take you about three hours for each film. (I like to save this exercise for Sunday nights; things are usually quiet after my Chargers have lost another football game.)

But you could space this out over a week.

Not only will this make your knowledge of film structure way more intuitive, but also it will boost your confidence in talking about what works and doesn't work, in your own scripts.

I know. This sounds like a total pain in the ass. But if you do nothing else in this book, try this out for a month.

This is like getting an advanced film degree, without all those pesky Stafford loans.

"Son, You Got a Panty on Your Head"

Another riff on this exercise is one that comes from the awesome, and dearly missed, screenwriting guru, Blake Snyder, in his imminently readable book, "Save the Cat."

In it he describes putting the AUDIO of his

favorite movies and then driving around listening to them over and over again.

These work great for dialogue-heavy movies, like comedies. (Not so well for Michael Bay films.) I drove around for a month listening to nothing but "Mrs. Doubtfire" audio. (I learned more about writing jokes from that then I did from four years of film school. Maybe I should ask for a refund.)

You COULD also watch, or listen, to DVD commentaries. Though I try to avoid the ones by directors.

Directors are...how can I say this nicely?...ego-maniacal pricks who mostly care about a specific shot or which deleted scenes they had to cut.

Unless the director ALSO wrote the screenplay, stick with writers and producers. They provide the best insight — and the best gossip — on the hard creative choices that helped make the end product that made it to the public.

And if you want to listen to an absolutely, insane (and hysterical) commentary check out the one for the film "Airplane." (You might not learn much in terms of structure — that film isn't really about structure — but you'll be laughing the whole 82 minutes.)

Chapter 5 Key Takeaways:

- Watching a movie with a printed screenplay in your hand is the best film school you can attend. Look for how the writer handled locations, exposition and characterization.

- Listening to the raw audio of films can be helpful. Especially for dramas and comedies. (Not so much for movies where shit blows up.)

- DVD commentaries, especially of writers and producers, can be good too. Skip director commentaries.

Chapter 6:
Rewriting for People Who Hate Rewriting

"The rehearsal is the work. The performance is the relaxation."

-Constantin Stanislavski

I don't spend a lot of time in this here book telling you how to write your actual script.

That's because I believe writing a first draft is a crazy, insane, right-brained activity. (And all that fantastic theory and story structure can often HURT more than it helps.)

Yes, your screenplay needs structure. Yes, it needs organization. And set-ups and payoffs. And foreshadowing.

But you know what else it needs? Originality. Passion. Emotion.

Lots of you!

And the best way I know how to get more YOU in your script is to pound your way to the end of your script and THEN go back and add all that lovely organization and structure. (We went over the elements of screenplay structure you need to get started in Chapter 2.)

While you're going to movies and listening to DVD commentaries and reading screenplays cover to cover…

It's important to write one page after another. Until you've got 85-105 of the worst pages every written.

And once you've done that it's time to turn that bag of shite into cinematic gold.

"Feel Lucky, Punk? Well, Do Ya?"

So, how much rewriting SHOULD you do?

A good rule is to have nine or ten good, quality rewrites on your script.

And this isn't futzing with the names of your characters or rewriting your scene descriptions over and over until you've got that prose about your hero's rocket launcher just right.

You're going after the big fish. Making sure all the points connect. Ensuring the vision in your head, as best as you can, is represented on the page.

There are entire books devoted to rewriting your script. (Tom Lazarus's Rewriting Secrets for Screenwriters, (http://scriptbully.com/rewriting), is one of my favorites. I highly recommend you pick up a copy.) So I'm not going to try to replicate that much depth of material here.

But here are key tips in regards to rewrites:

Rewrite Tip No. 1: Make Sure Every Scene Builds Toward a Sequence

Remember what I mentioned earlier: *Make something happen every 10 pages.*

It's important every scene you write build toward "something" just around the corner. (Not a resolution that's 40 pages away.)

It could be:

- A showdown
- A kiss
- A Stormtrooper shooting some Ja-Was
- Your hero breaking out of Shawshank

Have each scene build until it reaches a sequence climax. Then rinse and repeat. Obviously some sequences will be more important and dramatic than others.

In "When Harry Met Sally," the sequence that ends with him discovering she's going on a date with another guy is NOT as significant as the one that ends with them sleeping together.

But if you give each sequence a beginning, middle and end, you'll get a feel for where the big events NEED to happen.

The big mistake most screenwriters commit is they write a scene on page 20, hoping it will pay off on page 100.

Sorry! This iPhone generation won't get to page 100. Or page 20, unless your scene builds momentum toward something much closer at hand.

Rewrite Tip No. 2: Take Your Act-II Climax and Move it Back 20 Pages

I know. Sounds impossible. I mean, how can I possibly make you do this?

But trust me, moving your climax back will not only improve the pacing of your script (big time!), but it will also force you to come up with an even better ending to your film.

And I just know you've got a bigger, more awesome ending in you somewhere (The ending to "Casablanca" was rewritten seven times. The original ending to "Fatal Attraction" had Glenn Close's character commit suicide.)

You can do it. If you push yourself.

Speaking of endings…

Rewrite Tip No. 3: Make Sure Your Ending Has Resonance to Your Beginning

I hate it when movies don't do this. When the end of a film doesn't point back to the beginning of the film.

And it's so easy. (Not to mention super-effective.)

Because it makes the audience feel they've come full circle. (Like giving them a medal for sitting and watching your crazy characters whine for 90 minutes.)

And it can be virtually anything:

- An image
- A piece of dialogue
- A physical object

- A gesture

Something that was there in the beginning, and is now echoing in the end.

But make sure the payoff you're using to point back to the beginning is "the same, but different." It must have a different feel or meaning than it did in the beginning of your script in order for this to be effective.

Dorothy returns to family farm in Kansas at the end of "The Wizard of Oz." But NOTHING is the same. (She's wiser, older, and aware she doesn't have to leave her rural black and white world to find technicolor magic and belonging.)

John Wayne stands in the doorway of the Edwards' cabin at the end of "The Searchers," an image that cropped up in the beginning of the film. But he's not the confident, rugged gunslinger anymore — instead we sense the isolation and disconnect he feels from the very people he tried to save.

Woody Allen in "Hannah and Her Sisters" - in what I would argue is his best film - begins and ends the script with Thanksgiving parties at Hannah's house. But so very much has changed. (Including who each of the sisters is married to.)

Rewrite Tip No. 4: Break Up Your Rewrites By Topic and Character

Once you've got the major heavy lifting of your story out of the way - what your ending is, the order of your scenes, which characters need to go away and die - then you can REALLY start the rewriting process.

And this is my *favorite part of writing a screenplay*.

Yet so many writers dread it; I think it's because they get buried in the weeds and get totally overwhelmed.

I like to combat this "overwhelm" by making sure each rewrite has a specific function.

Your first rewrite can be focused on sharpening your dialogue. The second on making sure the ends of your scenes end with a BANG. Another focused on location. Still another focusing squarely on your romantic lead...you get the idea.

If you're trying to fix everything in your script all at once, you'll be miserable. (And get nothing done.)

But by focusing on just one area you can be way more productive in a fraction of the time.

Chapter 6 Takeaways:

- Churn that first draft out! Let the rewriting process add all that heavy-duty screenplay structure crap.

- When rewriting make sure each scene builds to a sequence. Break each sequence into a beginning-middle-end to keep your story on track.

- Push your MONGO Act-II climax back 20 pages and then come up with an even bigger climax. This'll help give your Act-II some much-needed acceleration and tension.

- Try to have your ending call back something from the beginning of your script. Could be an image, a piece of dialogue — whatever! (Don't deprive your audience of this super-fun treat.)

- Devote each rewrite to a specific area of emphasis. Whether it be locations, snappy dialogue or supporting characters, focusing your rewrites this way will avoid you rewriting the same paragraph 22 times.

Chapter 7:
Moving to L.A. (If Only In Your Mind)

"Bite off more than you can chew, then chew it."

-Courage Wolf

Don't worry.

You don't have to start looking for Malibu real estate that'll eventually fall into the ocean.

Yet.

This is about being PERCEIVED as an industry professional. And I know it's superficial and shallow.

And I know your marketability should be judged on your merits alone. And silly things like which zip code you call home shouldn't matter.

But Hollywood has never been known as a bastion of enlightenment.

So, here are my THREE Killer Tips for becoming a cool L.A. screenwriter without packing up a single U-Haul box.

Movin' to L.A. Tip No.1: Get an L.A. Phone Number

When you're an established screenwriter, you can live in a bear hut in Yosemite and nobody will care.

As long as you deliver great pages.

But until you sell your first mid-$300,000 script, you'll have to hustle and pretend like the rest of us that you're way more connected than you actually are.

So to perpetuate that valuable ruse, it's important to get a contact number producers and managers can reach you at that doesn't scream the fact you live in

Podunk Falls, Michigan.

Even if you live in Podunk Falls, Michigan.

And you do that by having an L.A. phone number.

But, how do we get an L.A. number...you know...without moving to L.A.? Easy.

Google Voice is a great tool that lets you sign up for a phone number and choose your area code. It's free, it transcribes your calls, and you can have it dial over to your primary number.

Just be sure to go with a 310, 424 or 213 prefix. (949 is Orange County, so forget about that.)

Another bonus is it can act as a super quick writing dictation tool.

Just call the number, leave a message and it'll send you an email message with a transcription of what you said.

If anybody says, "But I thought you lived in L.A." Just tell them you're out of town on assignment. (You don't have to tell them that assignment is living in your parent's basement in Michigan.)

Movin' to L.A. Tip No.2: Learn the Lay of the Land

One more thing that'll really help your L.A. street cred is to…well…learn L.A.

There's nothing producers, managers and agents love to bitch about more than the City of Angels. (And it's horrible traffic and scorching heat and shallow, ruthless ambition.)

And that it takes FOREVER to get anywhere around this town. (Especially when shuttling between the studios.)

It's good to know:

Universal Studios is up in the north, near Studio City.

Disney and Warner Brothers are east of Universal, in Burbank. (Lot of television production there too.)

Paramount Studios is in central Hollywood, near Sunset Boulevard.

And… far west, in wealthy Century City (where the agents work), is Fox Studios.

Here's a <u>handy little map</u> to help you visualize things in the Southland.

I know you don't live here. (Yet.) I know you may hate Los Angeles with a passion. (Me too.) But learning the geography of this town will not only help you establish rapport with industry decision makers…

But it will also boost your confidence and make you feel like an insider. (Which can see you through to the end of a long screenwriting project.)

Movin' to L.A. Tip No.3: Go Old School

I'd like you to think about becoming a STUDENT of classic Hollywood.

And that means classic Hollywood films. And classic Hollywood stars.

And classic Hollywood stories about that one famous (bitchy) actress trying to kill that other famous (bitchy) actress. (Yes, I'm talking to you, Joan Crawford and Bette Davis.)

The one perfect icebreaker I have found, no matter what part of the business I find myself in, is stories about classic Hollywood. (And which studios were trying to screw over which amphetamine-infused actress in the old days.)

When you make a comment that shows you care about movies made before the dawn of Twitter that you actually appreciate the history of this business — and the crazy/brilliant folks who built it from scratch — the more you'll ingratiate yourself to industry decision-makers. (Who love movies, despite evidence to the contrary.)

So watch those intros on TNT — you can skip the movie if you like, though I hope you won't — and collecting tidbits of Hollywood lore. (Another great resource is the podcast, "You Must Remember This," by Karina Longworth. If you want gossip-y knowledge about Hollywood's checkered past, this is a great tool.)

Who knows? You might pull one out during a pitch meeting which makes the difference between you selling a script for mid-$400K…and sitting at home in Podunk Falls waiting for the phone to ring.

Chapter 7 Key Takeaways:

- Sign up for a Google Voice account. Get your 310, 424 or 213 area code phone number and put it on all your contact info.

- Become acquainted with the geography of L.A. Learn where all the studios — and sections of the city — are located.

- Build up your classic Hollywood knowledge. Watch TNT intros and documentaries to get neat tidbits of Tinsel Town gossip.

Chapter 8:
Filling Your Little Black Book

"Real violence in Hollywood isn't what's on the screen. It's what you have to do to raise the money."

-David Mamet

The best time to look for a job is when you've already got one.

And the best time to compile your list of industry contacts is while you're writing your script, not after it's already done.

And the absolute best way I know how to do this is to compile a list of RISING TALENT in the industry you can contact at a later date.

"It's the Pictures That Got Small"

Notice I said "rising." Not established or Oscar-winning or retired or already awesome, so they don't need anything from you.

This is the often young - mostly emerging - actors, directors, producers, managers and agents who are on their way up the mountain, but need that "extra little push" that a smart, creative script can provide.

Your smart, creative script.

And when you look at the business through this lens, it's less of seeing the gatekeepers of the business as "doing you a favor"…

But instead a situation where they're given a chance to read your "intellectual gold" that can boost their career.

But before you reach out those decision-makers, you've gotta do your homework. And that means going to see movies before they come out on DVD.

That means checking out a film festival or two to find out who the hot directors and actors are

BEFORE they end up on TMZ.

That means paying attention to the credits of every movie you see to find out who that interesting supporting actress is, or which cinematographer wants to be a director someday, or which producer likes edgy films your script emulates.

Just be sure the contacts are working within your given genre.

There's no point in writing down the A.D. (Assistant Director) on "Transformers 3," if you're writing a 120-page script about Depression-era ditch diggers. (Unless those ditch-diggers happen to be robots.)

Other sources for compiling this talent include:

- Horror Movies: Today's slasher victim is tomorrow's Oscar-winning actress. Pay attention to young talent who have a clue what they're doing, but just need the right script to put it all together.

- Entertainment Weekly: Great for

scanning up-and-coming talent in the biz. Especially if you don't have time to see every movie on the planet. (Entertainment Weekly)

- Must-Read Blog: Another great online source is what Mark does over at "I Watch Stuff" (http://www.iwatchstuff.com/) Lots of great trailer info, and he usually has a good bead on what's shaking at all the festivals. (He was in on "Pan's Labyrinth" a full two years before anybody else was.)

- TV: Not great for finding directing talent, as TV is a writer's medium, but that supporting actress who's really under-utilized (I'm thinking of anybody acting opposite Kevin James) might love that quirky comedy written just for her.

- Opening Credits: Every film you watch has tons of good info. What to look for? I'd start with director, director of photography, producer, line producer, assistant director, and any actors and actresses that catch your eye.

Again, you're looking for ascending talent. Megan Fox could have used your script after her small role in "Confessions of a Teenage Drama Queen." But after "Transformers," it's too late. (Although the way her career is going....)

"Do or Do Not, There is No 'Try'"

So, you got names. Big deal!

What do you with them now? Once you've collected all these "names"—producers, directors and actors - who are ascending talent within your genre.

What good does that do you? Well, it tells you who you will be pestering with your email queries. And for that job, let me introduce you to my little friend: IMDb Pro.

"You've Got a Friend in Me"

If this were ten years ago, I would have suggested you buy a copy of the "Hollywood Creative Directory" (HCD).

But I also would have suggested you invest in MySpace and Friendster. (How things have changed.)

The "HCD" is kaput, a casualty of corporate takeovers and the internet. Luckily IMDb Pro has taken its place.

A subscription to IMDb Pro costs $124.95 a year (or $15.95/month) — well worth the price of admission to a full-time career as a screenwriter. (And really, if you have your names collected already, you should be able to get everything done within a single month.)

But if you're on an ultra-cheap budget, and being an aspiring screenwriter that may be likely, here's another way to go: the old "email address structure" gambit.

Let's say I want to reach out to Dirk Digler at Digler Talent Agency.

I would Google to find the email structure for the agency. (Such as jim@digleragency.com or Jim.Smith@thedigleragency.net, whatever.)

This can usually be done by getting the name of one agent or manager at a company. Then just Google: "email address" AND "Dirk Digler."

This will probably let you figure out how the IT department has set up their email format. Throw in the appropriate talent representative you are looking for and you're done.

And what do you do once you've got your contact info up and running? Well, you barrage the film business with your awesomeness…which is what we'll cover in the next chapter.

Chapter 8 Key Takeaways:

- Start compiling lists of agents, producer and managers connected to "ascending" Hollywood talent. Skip the A-list actors and shoot for the C- list starlets.

- Great places to find this talent are horror movies and film blogs like Now Showing. Don't forget opening credits to theatrical releases and cheesy TV shows where the actors are way more talented than the material they're presenting.

- IMDb Pro is a great investment to help you find the email addresses connected to that talent.

- If you're super broke, you could also use the sneaky email template approach. Find the email "structure" used by the agency or production company and then reverse-engineer your way to a usable email contact.

Chapter 9:
Crashing the Hollywood Party

"Sometimes you have to jump out the window and grow wings on the way down."

-Ray Bradbury

I know. Reaching out and conversing with humans is not part of our job description as screenwriters. (Caffeine-induced ulcers and a seething hatred for reality television are.)

But...

As you move from newbie scribe to well-paid screenwriter, I'd like you to embrace TWO forms of contact: One, letting people ALREADY in the industry know you admire their work, and two, sending email queries to your list of ascending talent to see if they'd be interested in your screenplay.

Both are important. Both will help you in your professional career.

And, both, are easier (and less terrifying) than you'd think. Let's take them individually.

Talking With Humans Method No.1: The Ultimate High Five

I can't prove this scientifically, but I don't think it's a coincidence I got my first screenplay option - this is where somebody gives you money to shop your script around town - soon after I started the "you rock" process.

Here's how it works:

Five days a week (see, I'm not such a bad guy, I'm letting you take weekends off), I'd like you to write a quick letter or email to a writer, director, author or actor whose work you admire. (Don't tweet, that's lame.)

It doesn't have to be twelve pages long. It doesn't have to be a seminar.

Just something that says:

"Hey, I saw this thing you did. It was awesome. It really touched me. You rock."

Something like that.

Don't ask for a favor. Don't ask them to read your script.

Don't ask them to introduce you to Charlize Theron. (Although if they do, email me. I'd love to tag along.)

The key is to just give them appreciation for what they do. In this business, it feels like everybody wants something from you.

I promise, a quick note to somebody saying their work is great will feel like a sign from God.

PLEASE be specific. Don't say your writing was great, say: *"That scene with the pretzel and the yo-yo, where Grandma confessed her love to Stalin. That shit made me cry."*

You may not get a response. That's okay.

They may file a restraining order. That's all right.

Just keep doing it.

My best experience with this was when I wrote screenwriter Robert Schenkkan after I saw "The Quiet American."

I was blown away by the restraint and beauty of the writing. I found out who his agent was, wrote him a note and Robert emailed me back. Turns out he wrote "Pump Up the Volume," one of my favorite guilty-pleasure movies. (I still have a dream of running a pirate radio station in my basement.)

We've emailed each other a few times over the years and I've never asked him for a favor. But it made me feel like a part of the professional screenwriting community. (And I got my first option soon after.)

Coincidence? I think not, Mr. Bond!

And if you believe in Karma or Mojo like I do, this whole "paying it forward" stuff can do nothing but put out good vibes in the universe.

And as writers, we'll take all the good vibes we can get.

Talking With Humans Method No.2: The Cold (Not so Cold) Email Query

Here's what you need to know about queries for screenplays: There are nearly 50,000 screenplays registered with the Writer's Guild every year.

And 99 percent of them suck.

Two of my notable sucky favorites I've read as a script reader include:

A script about a league of top-secret poets who go around the country decoding inner-city graffiti left by aliens.

A script where one of the members of a love triangle was dead. (Not a vampire. Not a member of the "undead." Not even a zombie. Actually lying-in-a-coffin dead.)

And then there are the countless number of projects which — while they don't technically involve felonies — do have banal dialogue, wooden characters and plot points so predictable they seem to have sprang out of a "Walker, Texas Ranger" marathon.

And these are from writers who actually have agents!

Then there's the drivel that ekes out of the many writer's groups and B-list contests and community college film classes around the country.

So...imagine if you were a producer working 14-hour days and trying to juggle 10 projects, 12 clients, and two alimonies…

Would you spend your weekend reading a 156-page script about midget snipers from a postman in Dover, Delaware?

Or would you rather read a 110-page script with a marketable premise from an industry professional?

The answer to that question is all you need to know about "breaking in" to Hollywood.

Golden Rule of Hollywood

They WANT to read great scripts.

But they don't want to WASTE THEIR TIME.

And, since most scripts SUCK, it's easier to assume that yours does too.

So they DON'T WANT to read your script.

But I know what you're saying...you're not in the business yet. You're not a professional, yet.

Yeah, but they don't have to know that.

"Open the Pod Bay Doors, HAL"

Because all you will do with your email query—yes, email, letters are dead—is pitch your story.

Not tell them about your degree from Wichita State, or that you've been writing scripts since the third grade...

...or that this is your nineteenth script or you have a "personal connection" to the world of competitive eating which makes you the best person to write this script.

Just pitch the story like you're in the business.

And how do you do that?

By taking a previously successful movie and giving it a spin.

An example using "Eagle Eye":

***

Subject Line:

"Available Thriller," "Available Comedy," or "Available Horror" or, if you're contacting a talent's manager or agent, "Re: Christopher Nolan"

Email Body:

"I have an available script.

It's "Conversation" meets "Enemy of the State" set in the world of satellites and surveillance.

Would you like to see it?

Michael Rogan
(310-225-xxxx)"

***

And that's it!

Don't break down the entire script. Don't tell them they can contact you. (They can. That's what the phone number is for.)

Don't tell them every act break in the script. Just give them enough to see if they want to know more.

"It's "Transformers" meets "Good Fellas" set in the world of bagel shops."

"It's "Slumdog Millionaire" meets "Steel Magnolias" set on the island of Alcatraz."

"It's "Hunger Games" meets "Sound of Music" set in an Amish community."

I don't know about you, but I would want to read those scripts.

"I've Always Depended on the Kindness of Strangers"

If they like the idea, they'll ask for a one-sheet (a breakdown of your script). This is a good thing.

This means they're intrigued, but don't want to commit to a date. Just yet. It's okay, you're flirting.

All you've gotta do is tell them a bit about your characters, the big fear/obstacle the main character has and list the big events that happen every 10 pages. Keep it to one page.

And for God sakes, whatever you do, don't pitch a story that involves Top Secret Poets.

Chapter 9 Takeaways:

- Writing to people whose work you admire is a great way to bust your way into the film community. Don't ask for anything. And be specific!

- Most registered scripts suck. So don't worry about the odds. By reading this book…you're already better!

- When writing email queries to agents, producers, and managers keep it short. No rambling. Get in and get out.

- Reference the "ascending talent" your project is perfect for. This will help it get through the slush pile.

Chapter 10:
We Don't Need No Stinkin' Permission

"If you're going to kick authority in the teeth you might as well use two feet."

-Keith Richards

This is the shortest chapter in the book. But it might be the most important.

All the things we've talked about so far have been about removing the (seemingly) impossible obstacles between you and an actual successful screenwriting career. ("I don't know what to write about," "I don't know story structure" or "I don't know a single soul in the film business so I might as well give up my dream and get a job in a call center.")

For me, and many writers I work with, there is this constant yearning for some authoritative voice in their life to say…"Damn right, you're good enough. Get out there and go for it!"

The problem is: that voice NEVER comes. (Or if it does, you won't believe the voice and you'll end up looking for "another" more authoritative voice to listen to.)

Because your friends and your family and your co-workers and your exes and the members of your writing group and that hipster down at the indie movie rental store don't think you can make it.

Not that they don't love you and support you and want you to succeed. They would just be a lot more comfortable if you chose something a little more secure.

Like advertising. Or real estate. Or bungee jumping.

Because let's get real: *nobody actually makes it in Hollywood.*

Except they do. All the time.

If you're waiting for that magical moment when the stars will align and you'll have plenty of money, time, confidence, sleep, energy, support and experience to make it work….

… you'll be waiting a long time.

Because this path is hard. And frustrating. And heart-breaking. And soul-achingly brutal. (And that's just finding a decent apartment in LA.)

And people who love you don't want you to suffer.

But what they don't realize is that if you don't do it, if you don't give it a serious go, then you'll suffer far more.

"I Got Rhythm, I Got Music"

My grandmother was born in 1900. She was 94 when she died.

In the 20s she spent her days singing in a Red Cross band, and her nights dancing in speakeasies.

(Amongst other things.)

Near the end of her life I asked her if she had any regrets.

"Should have sung more. Had lots more songs in me."

You got songs in you. Don't wait to sing them until you're 94. Do it.

Now.

Who knows, that song you've been excited/terrified to share with the world might just end up changing your life. (And the lives of the people who see your movie.)

Chapter 10 Takeaways:

- Managing doubt and self-sabotage is the number one skill pro screenwriters have. Everything else can be faked/learned.

- Don't wait for permission to GO after your screenwriting dream. Nobody thinks you can do it anyway, so fuck 'em!

Final Note…Or What the Hell Do I Know?

A couple of years ago, I was at a writer's conference and there was an uber-successful screenwriter who I went to high school with doing a panel.

I won't mention his name, but let's just say he wrote a pretty awful movie about an asteroid hitting the Earth while a band from Boston sang a song.

Anyway, I hated him.

My hatred ran deep. We had an English class together, senior year, and his writing was awful.

Worse than awful, it was boring AND awful AND he thought it was the best shit ever.

And now he was making millions of dollars with what I saw as less-than-mediocre talent, while I was getting paid 50 bucks a pop to read horrible scripts about alien strippers whose spaceship crash-lands in Moose Jaw, Canada.

So I introduced myself. Casually mentioned we went to the same high school. (Go Mustangs!)

And after some small talk — it was clear he didn't remember me — I blurted out, "Ya know, I was surprised you made it as a screenwriter."

He paused. Then replied, *"I wasn't. Guess that's why you're paying $300 to talk to me now."*

Ouch. He was right.

There are TONS of talented writers out there.

But it's the ones who keep writing — even when they feel like they totally suck and they're writing the worst shit on the face of the earth — who break through and get to write movies (about asteroids) that pay them close to $800,000.

Not that it's about the money, mind you. But...

Moliere, famous 17th-Century French playwright, once said:

"Writing is like prostitution. First, you do it for yourself. Then you do it for others. And then you figure, hell, I could get paid for this."

Here's hoping you stick with this crazy, but wonderful vocation. And keep writing. First for yourself, and then for others, till you get paid. A lot.

Good luck with your writing. And if you've enjoyed this book, drop me a line at Michael@scriptbully.com.

Thanks!

Appendix: Or All Those Resources We Mentioned

Chapter Three:

- "Moonstruck" – ScriptBully.com/moonstruck
- "Shawshank Redemption"- ScriptBully.com/Shawshank
- "Raising Arizona" – ScriptBully.com/Arizona

Chapter Six:

- "Rewriting Secrets for Screenwriters" – Scriptbully.com/rewriting

Chapter Seven:

- Google Voice – Google.com/voice
- "You Must Remember This" Podcast – ScriptBully.com/RememberPodcast

Chapter Eight:

- Entertainment Weekly - ScriptBully.com/eweekly
- I Watch Stuff – IwatchStuff.com
- IMdB Pro – ScriptBully.com/imdbpro

Don't Forget:
A Special FREE Gift for You!

If you'd like FREE instant access to my seminar "7 Secrets to a Kick-Ass and Marketable Screenplay" then head over to ScriptBully.com/Free. (What else you gonna do? Watch another "Twilight" movie?!)

DISCLAIMER AND/OR LEGAL NOTICES: Every effort has been made to accurately represent this book and it's potential. Results vary with every individual, and your results may or may not be different from those depicted. No promises, guarantees or warranties, whether stated or implied, have been made that you will produce any specific result from this book. Your efforts are individual and unique, and may vary from those shown. Your success depends on your efforts, background and motivation. The material in this publication is provided for educational and informational purposes only and is not intended as medical advice. The information contained in this book should not be used to diagnose or treat any illness, metabolic disorder, disease or health problem. Always consult your physician or health care provider before beginning any nutrition or exercise program. Use of the programs, advice, and information contained in this book is at the sole choice and risk of the reader.

CPSIA information can be obtained
at www.ICGtesting.com
Printed in the USA
LVHW082012010420
651875LV00009B/2757